The Buildings of Chester

1 The most photographed structure in Chester is probably not the cathedral, and certainly not the castle. The Rows around the Cross may been captured on many miles of film, but the Eastgate clock seems to sum up Chester for thousands of tourists. Perhaps it is an appropriate symbol, celebrating as it does the 1897 Jubilee of Victoria, during whose reign Chester took on its present appearance

The Buildings
of Chester

RICHARD K. MORRISS

With photographs by Ken Hoverd

ALAN SUTTON

First published in the United Kingdom in 1993 by
Alan Sutton Publishing Limited
Phoenix Mill · Far Thrupp · Stroud · Gloucestershire

First published in the United States of America in 1993 by
Alan Sutton Publishing Inc · 83 Washington Street · Dover · NH 03820

Copyright © text Richard K. Morriss
Copyright © photographs Ken Hoverd

British Library Cataloguing in Publication Data

Morriss, Richard K.
  Buildings of Chester
  I. Title
  720.942714

  ISBN 0–7509–0255–8

Library of Congress Cataloging-in-Publication Data applied for

Chester cathedral interior photographs by kind permission of the Dean and Chapter

Typeset in 11/14pt Times.
Typesetting and origination by
Alan Sutton Publishing Limited.
Printed in Great Britain by
Redwood Books, Trowbridge, Wiltshire

Contents

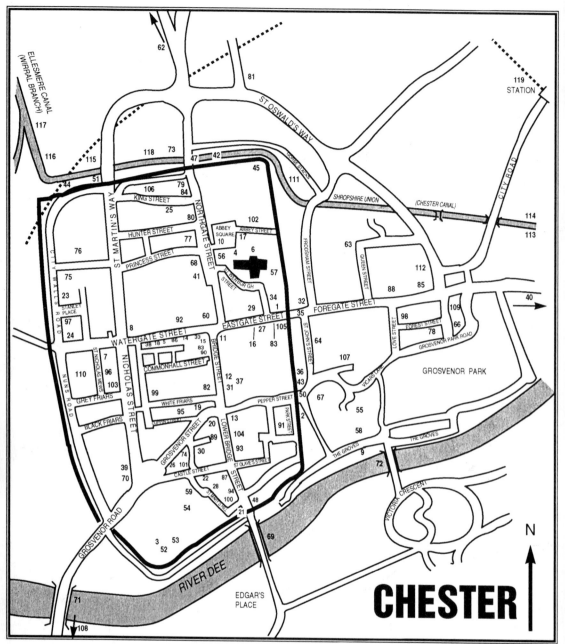

CHESTER

N

(Numbers relate to caption numbers in text)

Introduction

Chester, with its Roman street pattern, medieval town walls, castle, cathedral, and rows of timber-framed buildings, is one of the great historic show-pieces of England. The City figures prominently in the English Tourist Board's brochures, and attracts hundreds of thousands of visitors each year. It is, then, perhaps something of a surprise to realize that this essentially English place is only just in England – and that its western suburbs straddle the Welsh border.

This closeness to Wales is the reason for the town's existence. Situated at the head of the once much-wider Dee estuary and at the lowest crossing point of the river, Chester has always been strategically placed for those wishing to conquer or control North Wales. There was probably a Roman camp here as early as the late AD 50s. By the end of the 70s a much larger and permanent fort was established by the 2nd Legion – the *Adiutrix*. In AD 88 they were replaced by the famous 20th – the *Valeria Victrix*. The Romans called the place *Deva*, the 'divine', holding the river in the same reverence as the native tribe had done before them.

The regular and rigid plan of the standard Roman fort, known throughout their former empire, has left its mark on the modern city. Within the rectangular defences, the roads from the four gates met at the middle by the military headquarters, the *principia*. Running west to east through the town was the main street, the *via principalis*, marked by today's Eastgate and Watergate streets. Southwards from it, on the line of modern Bridge Street, was the other important street, the *via praetoria*. Northwards, along the line of Northgate Street, was the *via decumana* leading to what would have been the 'back-gate' of the defences. The original timber barracks were replaced by more substantial stone structures, and at the start of the second century AD the defences were refaced in stone. The garrison is estimated to have been capable of holding up to

2 Fragments of Roman Chester have been unearthed for centuries. Parts of Roman buildings still survive in cellars or buried deep and undisturbed below the city. These columns, made up of pieces from many different buildings, have been laid out in the Roman Gardens by the Newgate

6,000 soldiers. As well as the headquarters building and the barracks, the town also contained temples, bath houses, granaries and workshops. Just outside the east gate, or *porta principalis sinistra*, was the largest amphitheatre yet discovered in Britain.

Deva was always a military town, although there was some civilian settlement outside the east gate to serve the garrison, known as the *canabae*. Recent archaeological work shows that the base was not always fully occupied and several periods of rebuilding, especially in the early third and early fourth centuries, have been identified. In the late fourth century the legion was recalled to Rome in a vain attempt to prop up the empire. *Deva* was abandoned, and for 500 years seems to have sunk into oblivion.

The rural post-Roman society had no place for towns and no one seems to have occupied the deserted ruins. Chester was not forgotten, however, and must have been, even in its derelict

state, an impressive and emotive place for the warring Celts and Saxons. The Celts (or Britons) knew it as *Caerleon*, and the Saxons as *Legaceaster* – both meaning the 'city of the legions'. In about 616 King Aethelfrith of Northumbria defeated the Britons nearby, and the area was in Saxon hands by the mid-seventh century. Nevertheless Chester was still deserted in 893 when a Danish army camped within the walls for a short time. They saw it as a good base from which to attack Mercia. Perhaps it was this that led King Alfred of Wessex to realize just how important Chester could be, although it was his daughter, Aethelflaeda – the 'Lady of the Mercians' – who ordered extensive repairs and extensions to the defences in about 907. *Legaceaster* then seems to have grown remarkably quickly into an important regional centre, chosen as the county town of the new *scire* of Cheshire.

3 Chester Castle was founded by William the Conqueror to enforce his still tenuous rule over the English and to provide a base from which to control North Wales. The castle was rebuilt several times but still retained most of its medieval features when this engraving was made in 1786. Within a few years most of these had been swept away in a radical rebuilding programme

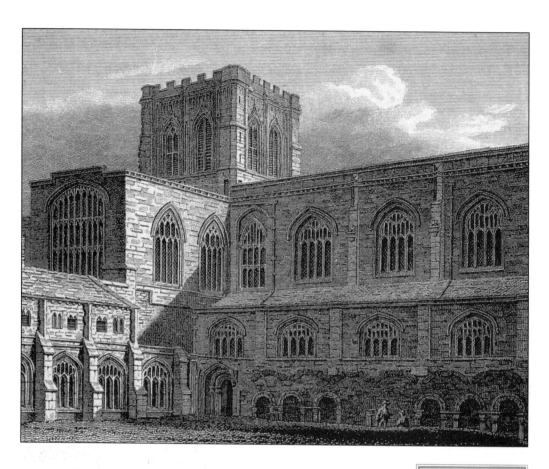

In 973 Edgar was, belatedly, crowned in Bath and recognized as king of all England. Tradition has it that he then sailed his fleet around Wales and up the Dee to Chester, where he had a palace on the south bank of the river – a site now called Edgar's Field. Eight subject kings rowed him from the palace across the Dee to St John's church and back in a display of loyal submission. By the Norman conquest *Cestre* was a busy port, the walls were being maintained, and the bridge had been built. It contained at least 500 houses, suggesting a population in the region of 3,000 – one of the largest in Saxon England.

The Norman hold on the north-west was at first tenuous, and in 1069 there was a general uprising that William the Conqueror ruthlessly crushed. Chester fell to William in 1070 and there is a laconic reference in the Domesday Book that when the city was given to Earl Hugh afterwards there were 205 fewer houses than

5 The appearance of Chester was altered dramatically in the late nineteenth century to produce the famous black-and-white townscape that today's visitors flock to see. In the eighteenth century the fashion was to cover up such old-fashioned work. This photograph of Bishop Lloyd's house, taken just before it was restored in 1899–1900, shows its old windows replaced by eighteenth-century sashes, and much of its fine carving covered by lath-and-plaster

6 The fourteenth-century shrine of St Werburgh, in the lady chapel, was heavily restored by Sir Arthur Blomfield in the 1880s. It is a rare survival, as most shrines like this were destroyed at the Reformation in the early sixteenth century. They had been built to attract pilgrims to cathedrals and monasteries alike, to help fill their coffers

there had been. Hugh d'Avranches, or Hugh Lupus, was the Conqueror's nephew and became Earl of Chester after the rebellion. He was given virtual autonomy in the new earldom, which stretched as far north as the Ribble estuary and west to the River Clwyd. It was effectively a buffer zone between the unruly Welsh and the more subdued English. Later known as a county palatine, it was ruled from the new castle built in Chester. Hugh also founded the great monastery of St Werburgh's, the present cathedral. In 1237 the earldom was annexed by Henry III, and after Edward I gave his eldest son the title it was by tradition given to the eldest son of the monarch – the present earl being Prince Charles.

Chester's importance grew during Edward I's campaigns against the Welsh at the end of the thirteenth century. It was in Chester that the English armies were mustered to attack the Welsh, and from its port these armies and the new castles along the coast were supplied. The castle was radically strengthened and parts of the cathedral were rebuilt. It was an important market centre and, bar Bristol, the busiest port on the west coast, specializing in the Irish traffic but also trading extensively with Gascony and Normandy. So prosperous was the city that, after a devastating fire in 1278, it was rebuilt in a very short time – a fact shown clearly by some of its architectural remains.

In the fourteenth century the city's fortunes began to wane. The Dee was beginning to silt up, and the onslaught of the Black Death in 1349 devastated Cheshire along with the rest of England. At the end of the century the Cestrians were loyal supporters of the soon to be deposed Richard II, and in 1403 they again chose the wrong side in supporting the Earl of Northumberland's revolt against Henry IV. By the 1440s the city's population was in severe decline, buildings were becoming derelict, and the estuary had become so bad that the ships were unable to get within 12 miles of the Chester quays. In the last years of the century it was claimed that as many as a quarter of the city's buildings were in ruins, and the walls were dilapidated. To make things worse, there were more fires in 1471, 1492 and 1494.

Despite being promoted by Henry VII, the first Tudor king, to county status in 1506, Chester's fortunes continued to suffer. Plague struck in 1507 and again in 1517, when the city was

6 The west door to the cathedral was part of the last monastic rebuilding, carried out in the early sixteenth century just before the Dissolution. Mercifully the street in front is cobbled, adding texture and complementing the ancient carved stonework

virtually deserted and grass grew high in its streets. Henry VIII closed the three friaries and the nunnery in 1536, and the great abbey of St Werburgh's was dissolved in 1541. The abbey church became the cathedral for one of six new dioceses created by Henry, one that originally stretched as far as modern Cumbria and North Yorkshire.

Slowly the city began to recover, and by the end of the century fine new timber-framed houses such as Stanley Palace were being built. By the early seventeenth century Chester was once again an important and prosperous place, and most of the surviving, genuine, timber-framed buildings date from this period. Sadly Chester again chose the wrong side in a national dispute – this time in the Civil War. King Charles arrived soon after raising his standard at Nottingham in 1642, sure of the city's loyalty. In the following months the walls were repaired, cannons

mounted on them, and new temporary outworks hurriedly constructed as the city prepared for the inevitable siege. Most buildings outside the walls were pulled down to improve lines of fire, including all the suburb of Handbridge. Several attempts to take the city were repulsed before Charles returned, in September 1645. From the walls, traditionally from the Phoenix Tower, Charles is said to have seen his army defeated on the 25th at Rowton Moor. On the next day he hurried over the Dee bridge, asking the city to hold out for ten days and then, if not relieved, to give in. Instead, proud Chester held out until 3 February 1646, surrendering with honour to the Parliamentarians.

The price paid was high. A contemporary account of the state of 'the most anchante and famous citie of Chester' lamented 'the ruines of it in these present times . . . the particular demolitions of it, now most grevious to the spectators, and more woefull to

8 The Old Customs House in Watergate Street, a reminder of the city's former status as a port, was built in a rather amateurish but full-blown Gothic Revival style in 1868. At the time it was described as 'a complete wart upon the beautiful church it adjoins'. Time, and the poor quality of its decorative stone, has softened its harsh lines

the inhabitants'. Due in no small way to the conditions endured during the long siege, a plague in the following year killed more than a quarter of the estimated population of 8,000. The city, no doubt, rejoiced at the restoration of Charles II in 1660, and slowly began to recover again.

In the eighteenth century attempts were made to revive the port by building a new, straight, channel in the estuary, a plan first put forward in 1677 but not started until 1732. Many, probably rightly, saw this more as an attempt to reclaim land for farming than a serious threat to Chester's former underport – Liverpool. Nevertheless, the port was revived to a degree, and by the 1770s ships of up to 350 tons were bringing to Chester linen from Ireland, flax, tallow, hemp and iron from the Baltic, and wine from Italy, Spain and Portugal. The main exports were coal and lead from the nearby mines of north-east Wales and

10 Abbey Square was laid out in the mid-1750s on the site of the bakehouse and brewery of the medieval abbey. Reached through the Abbey Gate it consists of two terraces of fine Georgian houses, all similar but not identical in design – one of the few examples in the city of a uniform layout. The column on the lawn is reputed to have come from the old Exchange

9 In the 1880s the riverside area upstream from the Dee bridge was refashioned as a park, having originally been laid out by Charles Croughton in 1725. In summer the Groves is an extremely popular venue, full of families watching the boats on the river and listening to brass bands. The bandstand is a principal attraction, a typical turn of the century structure of lacy ironwork cast by G. Wright of Rotherham

agricultural produce, such as cheese.

Chester was becoming a fairly fashionable place, frequented by the local gentry. The Groves were laid out by the river as a public park, and the walls, partially destroyed after the great siege, were repaired as a unique promenade around the city. New elegant brick houses were built, superseding the timber-frames of old, and assembly rooms were added to several of the better hotels to cater for the increasing social life of the well-to-do. In 1779 Boswell could write: 'here again I am in a state of much enjoyment . . . Chester pleases my fancy more than any other town I ever saw'.

At the turn of the century Chester's population was about 15,000, which had more than doubled by 1861 and, by 1900, had reached 38,000. This increase was not particularly great in comparison with the national average, mainly because Chester never really developed as a major industrial town – although its own industries were, indeed, important. These included the manufacture of clay tobacco pipes (for which it was nationally renowned), malting, flour-milling, dairy products, lead production and the railway works. Until the 1820s the city centre retained its Roman layout, but with the opening of the Grosvenor Bridge came the creation of Grosvenor Road, leading from the bridge to the city centre, cutting a diagonal swathe through the historic core. For the rest of the century the Grosvenors, of nearby Eaton Hall, dominated the life and architecture of the city, making it, for better or for worse, the place it is today.

Approaching the end of the twentieth century, Chester has a population of well over 80,000 and is busier than it ever has been. It is a thriving commercial, administrative and shopping centre, a commuter town for both Merseyside and Manchester, and one of the most popular tourist destinations in Europe. The pressures created by the needs of modern life on its architectural heritage are immense, but Chester seems to be coping better than most.

Architectural Character

Many visitors to Chester come because of its famous black-and-white timber-framed buildings, and many will go away again convinced that they have seen – and photographed – the architecture of old England. Yet Chester's architecture is a paradox. Most of the timber-framing that people see only dates from the 1880s to the 1920s. While most of these are bigger and bolder versions of older designs, others are almost exact copies, and many are the genuine article, radically rebuilt. Behind the thin veneer of Victorian and Edwardian Chester lies a rich architectural heritage seldom accessible to the general gaze.

No description of the city can avoid mentioning its unique medieval shopping malls – the famous Rows. At street level the shop fronts are fairly ordinary, and reached from the pavement. However, at first-floor level there is a second row of shops, set back and separated from the street by a covered gallery running inside the first floor of the buildings. For hundreds of years buildings that have come and gone, whatever their style, have respected this arrangement, and no other city has anything like it. The origins and the reasons seem lost in the mists of time. The architectural evidence of the oldest surviving features, and the more recent scientific evidence of dendrochronology – the counting of tree rings in original timbers – show that the layout of the Rows dates back at least as far as the thirteenth century. The basic pattern of each building is broadly the same. The ground floor is lower than the street level, and is reached down steps. Many

12 The ancient Rows of Chester, first-floor galleries running inside the buildings fronting the main streets, have long puzzled antiquaries. They are, quite simply, unique. This is part of the Bridge Street Row

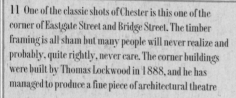

11 One of the classic shots of Chester is this one of the corner of Eastgate Street and Bridge Street. The timber framing is all sham but many people will never realize and probably, quite rightly, never care. The corner buildings were built by Thomas Lockwood in 1888, and he has managed to produce a fine piece of architectural theatre

ground floors are stone-vaulted, or at least stone-lined, and are often called crypts. On the first floor, between the gallery and the railings overlooking the street, is a raised sloping shelf, still used sometimes to display wares. Behind and above the shop at this level were the original domestic quarters of the owner.

The reason for the Rows' existence has puzzled historians for many years and a host of weird and wonderful theories have been put forward as well as more sensible ones. It has been suggested that when the Saxon settlement took place the ruins of the old Roman barracks and other buildings proved too hard to demolish. They were repaired, converted into useful store rooms, and new shops and houses were simply built above them, connected by a raised walkway. The other plausible theory is that, as Chester had suffered from

13 The early seventeenth-century Tudor House in Lower Bridge Street was restored by the city in the early 1970s. The Row once went through the building, but was built over in the early eighteenth century when the first-floor room was extended to the street – hence the brickwork and sash windows at that level

14 For at least 600 years the buildings lining Chester's main streets have respected the first-floor Rows. Apart from the Row, treated here as a Tuscan-columned arcade, this building of 1744 in Watergate Street is a typical mid-Georgian example – plain but elegant. The street level façade has been altered considerably, but at least its articulation matches the rest of the building

15 The left-hand building of this pair at the top of Bridge Street is an unusually unrestored seventeenth-century timber frame still as the Georgians left it. The front has been covered with lath-and-plaster and symmetrical sash windows have been added. Many of Chester's timber-framed buildings would once have looked like this. Beneath the contemporary, but restored, building of 1664 to the right is a magnificent thirteenth-century crypt

many fires in the twelfth and thirteenth centuries, it was decided after the blaze of 1278 to prevent such disasters. Owners were ordered to make their ground floors fireproof, leading to the building of the stone 'crypts'. These do seem to date from about this time, but others have been found in other towns in the Welsh Marches, such as Shrewsbury and Hereford. In each of those towns the 'crypts' are true under-crofts, below ground level, unlike their Chester counterparts. Quite why the Chester ones are not buried deeper in the ground is unclear, but it may have a strong bearing on unravelling the mystery of the Rows.

Today the Rows are part of Chester's many attractions and provide civilized covered shopping. The well-lit galleries are ideal places from which to watch the hurly-burly in the mainly pedestrianized streets below. They were not always well liked. Celia Fiennes, in 1698, wrote:

> The streetes are of a greate breadth from the houses, but there is one thing takes much from their appeareing so and from their beauty, for on each side in most places they have made penthouses so broad set on pillars which persons walk under covert . . . this does darken the streetes and hinder the light of the houses in many places to the streete ward below.

Daniel Defoe, about thirty years later, thought that they 'serve to make the city look both old and ugly'. Until the end of the nine-teenth century the Rows were neither particularly well-lit or well-kept. The only portion today that has anything like its early nineteenth-century character is the so-called Dark Row, on the north side of Eastgate Street.

The Rows apart, until the mid-nineteenth century Chester's architectural character was broadly similar to many other towns of similar size and antiquity in the region. The Romans had built in stone, and stone was still the usual material for the most important buildings until the late-medieval period – the castle, cathedral, churches, and walls included. Various fragments of Roman work can be seen re-erected in Northgate Street and the Roman Gardens, as well as in many basements and in the Grosvenor Museum. The local Bunter stone, a

16 Beneath the nineteenth-century Crypt Chambers in Eastgate Street is the original late thirteenth-century crypt that they were named after. This uses the most lavish arrangement of vault ribs in the city, accurately described by one historian as a Union Jack in stone. The well-preserved crypt is now a restaurant.

variety of New Red Sandstone, was being quarried by the Romans by the end of the first century AD, and the remains of their Handbridge quarry are still visible – protected by a shrine to Minerva. The medieval quarry that produced the stone for St John's church lies between it and the river, and is now a bowling green. The rich red stone is easy to work but very friable and prone to weathering, a fact seen all too clearly in the buildings made of it. Other local sandstones, with a greater variety of colour, came from the Keuper beds to the east of the city.

There is some evidence of domestic stone building in the medieval period, including the remains of a hall in Watergate Street, and the odd stone arches of part of the Row in Bridge Street, but most ordinary buildings of medieval Chester would have been timber-framed – and Cheshire was once a

17 In 1626 Bishop John Bridgeman had four cottages built for lay clerks on the site of the abbey's kitchen. These are rare examples of stone buildings dating from this time, but the stones were almost certainly reused from the demolished abbey buildings. Two still survive, just off the later Abbey Square

18 Bishop Lloyd's house, Watergate Street, is possibly the finest timber-framed house in the city. Built early in the seventeenth century as the home of a Bishop of Chester, it had become run down by the nineteenth. Its ornate carvings were hidden behind plaster and it was split into tenements, slowly becoming derelict. Saved and restored to its original form by Thomas Lockwood in about 1900, it was restored again between 1973 and 1977

19 In the mid-seventeenth century the panel infills between the timbers were sometimes decorated with ornate plasterwork, known as pargetting. The left-hand gable of No. 1 Whitefriars Street is dated 1658. The restored right-hand gable bears the date 1987. The jettied first floor looks almost like an afterthought to the original design

20 One-time home of the Grosvenor family, the Falcon in Lower Bridge Street was rebuilt in 1626. Below it is a much older crypt. Its splendid façade, which once had a Row passing through it, was restored by Grayson & Ould in about 1886. Virtually derelict by the 1970s, and propped up, it was restored by the city between 1979 and 1982 and the work won a Europa Nostra award in 1983

very well-wooded county. The timber-framed tradition lasted well into the late seventeenth century, at the end of which Celia Fiennes wrote that 'the town is mostly timber buildings'. These buildings were usually prefabricated, their timbers measured, sawn and temporarily slotted together in the carpenters' yards before being dismantled, transported to the site and re-erected. To make sure the pieces went together again in the right order, they would be individually identified with assembly, or carpenters', marks – generally a variety of Roman numerals. These marks can sometimes still be seen scratched or gouged into the timbers even after several centuries. The joints were usually mortise and tenons, held in place by thin pegs.

The early medieval frames had very large panels, but most of Chester's timber-framed buildings were built from the

21 The Bear and Billet, just inside the important Bridgegate, was rebuilt after the Restoration and bears the date 1664, thus being one of the last of the long line of fine timber-framed urban houses in England. Its long windows and ornately carved timbers are typical of Chester. One-time townhouse of the earls of Shrewsbury, who controlled the nearby gate, it later became an inn

late sixteenth to the mid-seventeenth centuries, when panel sizes were much smaller. They were filled with daub, a horrible mixture of dung, clay and animal hair, coated on wattles woven between vertical staves. Chester's own individual style of framing is extremely ostentatious, evolving very late on in the timber-framed tradition. It relies heavily on rich carving, ornate decorative panel timbering forming complex patterns, large expensive windows, and shallow-jettied upper floors supported on sculpted brackets. In Watergate Street the Stanley Palace of 1591 shows all these traits, as does the slightly later Bishop Lloyd's House. The Bear and Billet in Lower Bridge Street, built in 1664, is one of the last of the great timber-framed town houses in England.

Within a few years brick had become the only fashionable

22 This pair of late seventeenth-century brick houses, Nos 15 and 17 Castle Street, may have once been one large residence. There was once another 'bay' of windows and doors in the middle, now blocked. Note how, despite the use of fashionable brick, the old-fashioned gables of the timber-framed tradition were retained

23 Stanley Place is the most complete attempt at the type of uniform townscape made popular in fashionable places like Bath. Two parallel terraces of houses, built between about 1779 and 1781, front a long square. Even the gable ends are treated with some degree of unity, but oddly, the ground-floor layout of windows and doors does not match the floors above

24 Those who automatically associate Chester with black-and-white timber framing may be surprised to know that this typically Georgian view is of the bottom end of Watergate Street. The houses on the left were mainly built in the late eighteenth century. The church in the background is Holy Trinity, rebuilt in 1865-9 by James Harrison, and now the Guild Hall

25 Just out of the city centre, King Street is a little-changed Georgian backwater. It is good to see the cobbled road surface – though elimination of the single yellow line could improve it

material to build with, and flat, symmetrical façades were the architectural order of the day. If a completely new brick building was too expensive, a brick front tacked on to the older structure had to do. Those who could not afford even that simply covered the ornate timberwork with painted lath-and-plaster. In Castle Street is a late seventeenth-century brick building that still echoes the gabled fronts of the timber-frames. Later the gables were dispensed with, roofs were largely hidden behind parapets, and sash windows replaced casements. The rich red local bricks glow warmly in the sun-shine, a pleasant contrast to the mass-produced bricks that were brought into the city from the late nineteenth century onwards.

Because of the radical rebuilding of the city centre in the second half of the nineteenth century, it is now often difficult

26 Tudor Gothic was a forerunner of the timber-framed revival. James Harrison's Savings Bank is an extremely good example of the style, with good detailing, and clever massing of the main elements. It was built on Grosvenor Street in 1853

27 Between Thomas Penson's early attempts at timber-framed revival on one side, and his Gothic Revival Crypt Chambers on the other, is this much plainer building with Greek Revival Doric columns on the Row. It was built towards the end of the 1820s

to see Chester as the Georgian town it once was. Some fine terraces remain in Stanley Place and Abbey Square, and a few individual houses in the main streets also escaped the revivalists. Even so, too many of these have, alas, lost their original glazing bars and stare blindly at the onlooker with plate glass windows. Chester still has two grand examples of late Georgian architecture, both by the only important architect working in the town, and both built of stone. Thomas Harrison rebuilt the castle complex, a technically flawed but impressive early example of the Greek Revival style. It was he who also designed the Grosvenor Bridge, surely one of the most elegant in Britain. In contrast to his great works, Harrison's own house, St Martin's Lodge, is a modest Regency villa.

Neo-classicism continued in Chester until the mid-

28 The old rectory of St Mary's church was refaced in this neo-Tudor brick in the first half of the nineteenth century, a forerunner of the timber revival that was to come. St Mary's Hill has been restored and is a good example of urban conservation in action

29 George Williams's National Westminster Bank, on the corner of Eastgate and St Werburgh's Street, has giant Corinthian columns and a pediment, and is a very late example of neo-classicism. Built in 1860, just as the timber-framed revival was getting under way, the locals objected because it shortened the Row on that side of the street

nineteenth century, but there were already signs of the revivalism that characterized Victorian architecture – for example in the Gothic brick refronting of St Mary's Rectory, probably of the 1830s. In the second half of the nineteenth century most of the 'Georgianized' timber-framed fronts were restored to more or less their original appearance, and many Georgian buildings were demolished to make for new ones built in the old style. The earliest attempts at timber-framed revival were by Thomas M. Penson, and two of his earliest works survive in Eastgate Street. Penson was enthusiastic but not particularly careful in his work. His huge Grosvenor Hotel was a warning that this style was totally unsuited to large buildings – but the warning went unheeded.

Despite much opposition to the radical rebuilding of the

30 Preserving cobbled streets really does enhance the character of an area, and is seen to good effect in Grosvenor Place, a terrace of late nineteenth-century houses off Grosvenor Road. The houses are quite 'up-market' for such a late date

31 The original faience-faced front of St Michael's Buildings was disapproved of by the second Duke of Westminster and must certainly have been out of character with the rest of the street. The replacement mock-timber-frame is well balanced and not too overdone in its detailing, despite its huge size. It was, presumably, also by Thomas Lockwood and is one of the best in the city

32 As the timber-framed revival continued into the twentieth century, the buildings got even bigger but the historical accuracy deteriorated. The former District Bank (now the Royal Bank of Scotland), on the corner of Frodsham Street and Foregate Street, was built in 1921

34 St Werburgh's Street, with its terraces of gable-topped and jettied timber-frames, offers the finest view of the cathedral. Being Chester, it is not too much of a surprise that these were only built between 1895 and 1899. John Douglas bought the land, designing and building the houses on the right as a speculative venture. In doing so he created one of his best pieces of work

33 God's Providence House in Watergate Street shows just how radically the Victorians could 'restore' buildings. The original house was built in 1652 and the motto on the beam probably relates to its owners being spared from a plague. James Harrison virtually rebuilt the house in 1862, despite protests from local people, but retained one or two timbers

city, the influence of the Grosvenor family was everywhere. It was largely due to them that the Grosvenor Bridge was built, thus relieving the strain on the old one. Unfortunately, as part of the development a new road, Grosvenor Road, was built to link the bridge with the centre, cutting diagonally through the city. It took many decades before the road was lined with buildings. Richard Grosvenor, Second Marquis of Westminster, was a major influence on the city, but far more so was the Third Marquis, the first Duke of Westminster. From the end of the 1860s until his death in 1899 the Duke wielded paternalism and power, and certainly had the finances to do so: Eaton Hall was rebuilt, and a major pro-gramme of estate buildings started. The main architect involved was John Douglas, who proved to be extremely effective in the genre of the timber-framed revival and in the

35 The oldest visible structure in this view of the Eastgate from Foregate Street is the arch of the gate itself, built in 1769. The clock over it celebrates Victoria's Jubilee of 1897. The huge range on the left, Old Bank Chambers, was designed by Thomas M. Lockwood in 1895, and beyond the gate is T.M. Penson's Grosvenor Hotel of 1866

36 Baroque Revival in turn-of-the-century timber-framed Chester comes as something of a surprise, but a pleasant one. This range of 1908 is in St John's Street, close to the Roman amphitheatre

37 St Michael's Arcade, built in 1910 by Thomas Lockwood, was a logical extension to the first-floor shopping areas provided by the medieval Rows. It runs at right angles to Bridge Street. The glazed tiles – or faience – are typical of Edwardian Baroque, and originally the street front was faced with them

use of decorative brickwork. The other principal architect of the day was Thomas Lockwood, and both were heavily involved in the refacing of Chester.

Finding timber-framed façades that escaped the Victorians is not always easy, and the differences between the later versions and the genuine ones are sometimes difficult to spot. In general the copies are a little too crisp, and a little too good to be true. The 'frames' are often little more than planks nailed on to a brick carcass, and the pegs stick out too far. Above all, the later buildings are simply too big. Ironically, although much of the city's architectural heritage was swept away and replaced by facsimiles, this was all done with the best motives. A century of weathering has helped to tone down the Victorian and Edwardian magpie buildings and given them their own particular charm. Certainly Chester can lay claim to have the best examples of timber-framed revival streetscapes in the country.

Chester's council has shown itself to be keenly aware of the need to preserve its architectural heritage. Since the 1960s it has shown, by example, just what can be done by co-operation between a conservation-minded local authority and individual property owners. Many historic buildings have been saved from almost certain demolition in the process, and some good modern developments have taken place in the Rows and elsewhere. It is therefore something of a disappointment to see some of the other modern buildings that have been allowed. A lively and thriving place like Chester will always need to knock down some old buildings and build new ones better suited to modern needs; it will also need to expand. But these factors can never be used as excuses for bad architecture. Scale, proportion and materials are the key words, and some of the new developments in the city clearly measure up. Others do not, especially in the suburbs where bland brick housing schemes have sprung up, as they have done around virtually every other town in the country. People have to live somewhere, of course, so at least there are excuses for these estates.

Bad architecture seems far worse, and less excusable, in the middle of towns. Right in the middle of Chester, next to the

38 Modern buildings in the Rows have had to continue the ancient tradition of the first-floor shopping galleries. This example in Watergate Street dating from the 1960s might not be to everyone's taste, but at least the scale is correct and it respects its more elderly neighbours. Its façade is well-articulated, and it manages to contribute to the streetscape

39 Chester is lucky to still have the houses designed by its two principal architects for themselves, showing just how different their tastes were. Both, coincidentally, are now used as offices by the emergency services. Thomas Harrison designed St Martin's Lodge for himself in about 1820, when he was well into his seventies. It was built close to the castle complex that he had spent so many years remodelling. Elegant and simple, it is a fine understated piece of Regency architecture. It is used by the county police force

40 In complete contrast to St Martin's Lodge, John Douglas's Walmoor Hill in Dee Banks is a rambling and rather incoherent pile. Started in 1898, when he was in his late sixties, this L-shaped house was still unfinished at his death in 1911. It shows most of the typical Douglas details incorporated into a stone, rather than a brick or timber-framed, building. It is now used by the fire brigade

41 The Forum Centre, designed by Michael Lyell Associates at the start of the 1970s, may have sat perfectly happily in one of the New Towns then being created. Unfortunately it was built in the heart of one of the most historic cities in Europe, close to the cathedral and next to the Town Hall. Words are inadequate

Town Hall and opposite the Abbey Gate, is the front of the
Forum complex – perhaps the worst piece of modern urban
planning in the centre of any historic city in England.

Defences and Castle

Chester and York have the two best defensive circuits in England. York's circuit is slightly longer but slightly less complete – and only in Chester can the defences be circumnavigated on foot. The permanent fort laid out in the late 70s had the typical Roman 'playing-card' design – a rectangular enclosure with rounded corners. The north and east boundaries of the Roman fort were followed by the much later city walls. The west side was roughly on the line of St Martin's Street, Linen Hall Street and Nicholas Street, and the south side on Whitefriars and Pepper Street. Originally just turf ramparts topped by a timber palisade behind a ditch, they were refaced by stone walls shortly after AD 100. Repaired or rebuilt several times in the following 300 years, Chester's surviving Roman defences are some of the best preserved in Britain. They were built in good quality ashlar – far better, indeed than the later medieval masonry. The best stretch is just east of the Northgate, the Roman's *porta principalis decumana*, where the Roman wall is intact up to its original decorative cornice and the medieval wall is simply built on top of it. The footings of the south-east corner tower, built inside the angle of the walls just outside the Newgate, are also visible.

When Aethelflaeda reorganized the defences of the new Saxon *burh* in the early tenth century, she extended the defended area to the south and west as far as the lines of the present walls. In the late Saxon period it was the responsibility of the local authorities to maintain the defences and this continued to be the case after the Norman conquest. Most of the money to pay for the work came from *murage*, tolls charged on most goods

42 The best section of the Roman wall lies just to the east of the Northgate, overlooking the Chester Canal. Complete up to its ornate cornice, the fine ashlar of the Roman masons contrasts with the rougher work added on top of it in the medieval period

43 When the Saxons increased the size of the city in the tenth century, they abandoned the southern section of the Roman defeces. North of the Newgate are the remnants of the Roman south-east corner tower, built typically within the angle of the walls. The medieval wall is on a slightly different alignment. In the background is the fourteenth-century Wolfe, Thimbleby's, or Humphrey's Tower, badly damaged in the Civil War and restored in 1879

passing through the city gates. Chester continued to charge murage on some goods right up until 1835, which is one reason why it has managed to keep its wall circuit almost intact.

The walls of today mainly date from the thirteenth century but have been radically rebuilt and repaired on many occasions – originally for defensive reasons but later, in the eighteenth century, to provide a pleasant promenade around the city. None of the defensive towers look anything like they would have done originally, and many others have been lost. The most interesting tower, architecturally, was a later addition built as the estuary gradually silted up. In 1322 John Helpstone was paid £100 to build the New, or Water, Tower outside the north-west angle of the walls to help defend the port. It was connected to the angle tower by a spur wall with an arch over the tideway. This is now the most complete of the medieval towers, despite being restored

44 The Goblin Tower was called Dille's Tower in Tudor times. In the eighteenth century it was known as Pemberton's Parlour, because from it a ropemaker of that name used to watch his men at work in the yard below. In the early 1700s this stretch of wall was rebuilt, and the tower itself was remodelled in 1702. It was restored for a second time in 1894

45 King Charles was in Chester in September 1645 when his army was beaten by the Roundheads at Rowton Moor. Tradition has it that the king watched from the tower that now bears his name. Called the Newton Tower in medieval times, it was renamed the Phoenix Tower at the start of the seventeenth century when it was restored. Restored again in 1658 to take its present form, it now houses a small Civil War museum

46 At the north-west corner of the defences is Bonewaldesthorne's Tower. As the Dee silted up and the harbour moved further away from the walls, a new tower was built in 1322 and connected to the defences by an embattled spur wall. The Water Tower is probably the least altered of the medieval towers of Chester

several times; the spur wall was rebuilt as early as 1730.

In 1676 the cartographer John Speed wrote: 'in a long Quadren-wise the walls do incompass the City, high and strongly built, with four fair gates opening into the four winds, besides 3 posterns and seven Watch-Towers extending in compass 1940 paces'. All the medieval gates were pulled down in Chester, as in so many other defended towns and cities, in the late eighteenth or early nineteenth centuries to improve traffic flow. Of course the splendid thing about the good citizens of Chester is that they bridged these gaps in the circuit to save their precious promenade – and this tradition continued when first the railway, and later the inner ring road, breached the defences. Still called 'gates', these bridges are of a variety of styles and form a unique architectural collection. The oldest is the Eastgate of 1769, built by an unknown architect at the expense of Lord Grosvenor, but

48 The medieval Bridgegate was pulled down in 1781 and replaced by this plain but elegant affair in 1782. It was designed by Joseph Turner. Nearby was a later opening in the walls, the Shipgate, taken down in 1831 and later re-erected in Grosvenor Park

49 The Watergate, built in 1788 was, like the slightly earlier Bridgegate, designed by Joseph Turner. As its name indicates, it led down to the old port when the Dee still flowed alongside the city walls

50 The Wolfe's Gate was proving to be a bottle-neck to modern motor traffic in the late 1920s and it was decided to build a new, wider opening in the walls next to it. The Newgate, designed in a quasi-medieval style by Sir Walter Tapper, is built of reinforced concrete faced with Runcorn stone, and was opened in 1938

51 St Martin's Gate is the latest of the 'gates' in Chester's walls, built to allow the inner ring road through. Opened in 1966, it was designed in a very modern style jointly by A.H.F. Jiggins, City Engineer, and Grenfell Baines of the Building Design Partnership

by far the best is Thomas Harrison's Northgate, an elegant Doric design finished in 1810. The most recent is St Martin's Gate, built across the inner ring road in 1966 and a fine modern contribution; it is a shame that the same ring road is not bridged as it passes the castle, leaving wall-walkers to the mercy of a pelican crossing.

Chester Castle was started on the order of William the Conqueror after the rebellion of 1069–70 and was built by Hugh Lupus. Improvements were made in the twelfth century and then it passed to the Crown with the earldom in 1237. The royal castle was radically remodelled between the 1280s and 1320s by Richard the Engineer, as part of Edward I's campaigns against the Welsh. Richard, incidentally, was one the leading military architects of his day and a wealthy man. He lived in Chester and owned the fisheries and mills. The castle was considered a

strong and secure fortress for several centuries. Many trouble-makers were confined within it over the years, from Welsh rebels in the thirteenth century to Jacobites in the early eighteenth. Little is left of the 'strong and stately Castle, round in form' seen by John Speed. The earliest surviving feature, apart from the earthworks, is the twelfth-century Agricola's Tower. This was originally the gatehouse between the large outer bailey to the north, and the inner bailey to the south. On the first floor is a small late twelfth-century chapel, St Mary de Castro, with two bays of fine early rib-vaulting. Sometime in the thirteenth century the gateway was blocked, and the ground floor vaulting was rebuilt after a fire in 1302. From the seventeenth century until 1909 it was an ammunition store, and it was partially refaced by Harrison in 1818. The surviving walls of the inner bailey were largely rebuilt in 1786 and there are only fragments of the two

53 Agricola's Tower is the oldest surviving part of the castle and dates from the twelfth century. Once the gatehouse between the outer and inner courts of the castle, it was later altered when a new gatehouse was built. It was saved from demolition in the late eighteenth century, being repaired and partley refaced by Thomas Harrison. It contains the fine first-floor chapel of St Mary's de Castro

other surviving towers, the Flag Tower and the Half Moon Tower.

The reason for the lack of medieval features was the radical rebuilding of the castle carried out by Thomas Harrison for nearly forty years from 1785. Harrison won a competition to provide new buildings on the castle site for the county. The main buildings – a Shire Hall, Barracks, and Armoury – lie on three sides of a huge square, reached through a ceremonial entrance block on the fourth. The first part to be built was the Gaol, behind the Shire Hall and now demolished. In 1791 work began on the Shire Hall, which has a magnificent semicircular chamber with coffered ceiling and Ionic columns. Its portico was only started in 1797. The Barracks, to the left of the square, and the matching Armoury, to the right, came next, in 1800. The Greek Revival entrance, called a *propylaea*, consists of a Doric gateway flanked by pedimented lodges. It was only begun in 1810 after Harrison had made frequent changes to his designs, and took twelve years to finish.

Churches

Roman Chester would have had many religious buildings, ranging from small personal altars and shrines to large civic temples. Fragments of these now rest in the Grosvenor Museum. One shrine remarkably has survived more or less intact. The quarry workers on the opposite bank of the river carved a statue of Minerva in relief in the rock face, and this has survived centuries of erosion and vandalism. It is thought that in medieval times the people considered it to be a statue of the Virgin Mary, so left it alone – though how it survived the zealous Roundheads after the Civil War is less clear.

One of the many religious sects in the garrison may well have been the early Christians, but the first confirmation of their existence in Chester is not until the Saxon period. Several churches were founded then – including St John's, where excavations have uncovered Saxon crosses. One curious feature of these churches is their relationship with known Roman landmarks. St John's is outside the Roman walls but close to the amphitheatre; St Peter's, in the middle of the city, is virtually on top of the Roman *principia*; Holy Trinity is on the site of the Roman west gate; and St Michael's and the lost church of St Bride's both stood close to the site of the south gate. Perhaps these churches originally used Roman ruins in their construction.

Chester has the rare distinction of having had two cathedrals, and the oldest is often overlooked by visitors. The Saxon church of St John the Baptist was collegiate – that is, it supported a 'college' of secular canons. The Normans reorganized most aspects of English life, including religion. One edict decreed that cathedrals had to be located in the larger towns, and so in 1072, Bishop Peter, of the ancient Mercian see of Lichfield, moved to Chester and made St John's his cathedral. He set about rebuilding it, but died in 1085. His successor carried on the work but in

1102 moved to Coventry, at the opposite end of the diocese. Work on St John's seems to have stopped, but the magnificent Norman arcades give some idea of how ambitious a church it was to be. Work restarted a century later. From the outside the heavily restored appearance of the present church is, frankly, disappointing – the only interest really being in the ruins of the former east end left isolated from the main church. Inside, however, there is a rich lesson in architectural history. The solid late eleventh-century arcades with their round piers and round arches are about a century older than the triforium arches above, and the top row of arches, the clerestory, is slightly later still. When the college was closed at the Dissolution the church was threatened with demolition but, because the nave had been used as a parish church, it was saved.

It was the Dissolution that led to the establishment of

55 The Saxon church of St John's was chosen as Chester's first cathedral in 1072, and a major rebuilding scheme began. At the Dissolution much of the east end and the transepts were abandoned, including the lady chapel and the fourteenth-century choir chapels, and fell into ruin. The bell tower is Victorian, replacing an earlier tower at the west end that fell in 1881

55 The splendid interior of St John's can only give a limited idea of how grand this church must once have been. The three tiers of arches date from three different periods of construction – with the Norman work of pre-1100 in the round-arched arcades, the pointed triforium arches of about 1200 above those, and the clerestory dating from the mid-thirteenth century

6 St Werburgh's cathedral is best seen at night, under floodlights, when the dark dull sandstone is subtly lit. Heavily restored many times, this former monastic church became Chester's second cathedral in 1541. Its main delights lie within

56 The main entrance to the monastery precinct was through the Abbey Gate. The present archway is of mid-fourteenth-century date, flanked by niches that once contained religious statues. The first floor is a late Georgian addition

Chester's second, and present, cathedral – St Werburgh's. Werburgh, or Werburgha, was the pious daughter of a seventh-century Mercian king. Tradition has it that her remains were given to the church of St Peter and St Paul in Chester in 875 by the nuns of Hanbury, to save them from the Danish invaders. In 907 the church was re-dedicated to St Werburgh; by this time it was also collegiate. In 1093 Hugh Lupus turfed out the canons and established a Benedictine monastery with the help of Anselm, Abbot of Bec, in Normandy. Hugh Lupus died in 1101 and was buried in the abbey. It was this foundation that was closed on the orders of Henry VIII in 1541, and reopened as the cathedral of a new diocese.

Externally this great church is a little gloomy, mainly because of the dark stone. In 1798 it was described as 'one of the most heavy, irregular and ragged piles', and it certainly does lack

6 Before Romeo and Juliet became well known, the most famous medieval romantic pair were Tristram and Iseult. In this carving the two lovers are being spied on by her husband, King Mark. Needless to say, most versions of the story had an unhappy ending

6 The knight in armour is obeying medieval advice. If after capturing a tiger cub the tigress chases you, drop a crystal sphere and the tigress will see her reflection in it, think it is the cub and stop. The parable was a warning against the pursuit of frivolity

6 The elephant and castle bench end would have been carved by a craftsman who had never seen an elephant. One had been brought to England in 1255, a gift to Henry III by Louis IX (St Louis) of France, and it is likely that for over a century or more all other elephant carvings were based on ones made of that animal

much of the architectural consistency of many other cathedrals. Internally the church is also rather dark, thanks to the dull stained glass. Little early work is visible, apart from some Norman masonry in the north transept, that is probably contemporary with the work in St John's. The bulk of the church, however, is of fourteenth-century date; Richard the Engineer may have built the choir in the early part of that century. The pride of the church is its fittings – the unique shrine to St Werburgh, heavily restored but essentially of fourteenth-century date, and, above all, its magnificent choir stalls with their excellent misericords. The novelist Henry James was inspired by 'the vast oaken architecture of the stalls, climbing vainly against the dizzier reach of the columns'.

The cathedral has suffered from its four major restorations in the nineteenth century – by Thomas Harrison in 1818–20,

6 The mythical unicorn was an elusive and fierce creature. Yet if, on the off chance, the animal saw a pure virgin sitting alone in the forest, it would walk up to her and lay its head on her lap. In this scene the animal has been cruelly tricked and captured – symbolizing Christ's arrival in the world by way of a virgin, and his death at the hands of man

6 A husband being berated by his nagging, and in this case obviously rather violent, wife is a common subject for misericords. All the craftsmen were men, of course, and this was long before the days of equality. Perhaps the idea was to show the monks that they were better off in the monastery than outside it

6 It is always so satisfying to see old buildings being used for the purpose for which they were intended. The refectory was the monks' dining room. Up until 1876 it housed the King's School, and now serves as a very pleasant cafeteria and function room. The east window was rebuilt by Sir Giles Gilbert Scott in 1913, and the magnificent medieval-style hammer-beam roof was built by F.H. Crossley as recently as 1939

6 The refectory today is filled with the gentle chatter of visitors and other refugees from the busy city outside. In monastic times there was silence – except for the voice of one of the brothers reading from the Bible in the refectory pulpit. This was built at the very end of the thirteenth century and reached by an arcaded stair

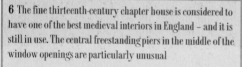

6 The fine thirteenth-century chapter house is considered to have one of the best medieval interiors in England – and it is still in use. The central freestanding piers in the middle of the window openings are particularly unusual

R.C. Hussey in the 1840s, Sir George Gilbert Scott between 1868 and 1876, and Sir Arthur Blomfield in the 1880s. This work was not done purely for the sake of it; the cathedral was in danger of collapse. Scott wrote that it was 'so horribly and lamentably decayed as to reduce it to a mere wreck, like a mouldering sandstone cliff'.

In contrast to the church itself, the former monastic buildings are a real delight. Chester is indeed fortunate in having an almost complete collection. The cloisters were mainly rebuilt just before the Dissolution, and again in the nineteenth-century, but several Norman doorways have survived. In the west range is an early twelfth-century undercroft and St Anselm's chapel. The chapter house, built before 1250, is a somewhat plain rectangular structure with tall lancet windows. However, it has one the finest vaulted interiors of its type, a splendid example of the first period

57 Looking rather like a cross between a disused windmill and a 1950s space rocket, George Pace's Addleshaw Tower was opened in 1975. It is claimed to be the first detached bell tower, or campanile, to have been built for a cathedral in this country since the Middle Ages – but not too many were built then either

of native Gothic architecture – the Early English. Perhaps even more exciting is its vestibule, whose clustered shafts around the piers rise and spread into the vault ribs without being hindered by capitals, generating a tremendous feeling of vitality and movement. The last, but by no means the least, of the major monastic survivals is the Norman refectory, happily now in use once again for its original purpose – and one of the most pleasant places for a quiet snack in the city. It was remodelled at the end of the thirteenth century, when its pulpit was added, and restored at the beginning of the twentieth. The cathedral's most recent claim to fame is in constructing the first detached bell tower for a British cathedral since the Reformation. In the late 1960s the bell frame in the great tower was causing concern, and it was decided that it would be easier to build a new, detached, tower rather than repair the old. The resulting Addleshaw Tower, 86 ft

58 The Anchorite's Cell is an architectural oddity. Tucked away in the quarry below St John's church, it was traditionally the place where King Harold retreated to after his defeat at Hastings. Any medieval work it does have is certainly much later, and it has been radically restored. An anchorite locked himself away from the world to concentrate on prayer

high, is built of concrete and brick, and faced with Bethesda slate. Finished in 1974 it is, to say the least, unusual.

Chester, like most medieval cities of its size, had several other religious houses until the Dissolution, including those of the Greyfriars (the Franciscans), Whitefriars (Carmelites) and Blackfriars (Dominicans), as well as St Mary's, a Benedictine nunnery. Nothing survives above ground, although a fragment of the nunnery was re-erected in Grosvenor Park and seems to be of thirteenth-century date. Otherwise only the names of the streets in the south-west quarter of the town commemorate these lost orders. One unusual building with some religious origins is the much rebuilt Anchorite's Cell, built in the quarry near to St John's. This little stone building has more to do with Romantic whimsy than medieval anchorites, but there may be some original work in it. One legend says that King Harold escaped death

59 St Mary's-on-the-Hill was built next to the castle. Although it dates back to Norman times the earliest visible remnants are the fourteenth-century arches of the chancel, and the church is mainly fifteenth- and sixteenth-century. It has been restored many times since; the upper part of the tower, for example, was added by James Harrison in 1862. It has been redundant since 1972 and is now used as an educational resource centre

60 Built close to the site of the Roman headquarters building, where the four main streets met, St Peter's is a church with a rich history but indifferent architecture. Although it has medieval features it has been radically rebuilt so many times that these are hardly in evidence. At one time its tower was crowned by a spire

61 The small medieval chapel of St Olave in Lower Bridge Street has always been a rather neglected and unwanted church, its tiny parish probably smaller than the cathedral precincts. Dedicated to an eleventh-century Norwegian king, it is a reminder of both Chester's links with Ireland, and the fact that Dublin was once a Norse city. It was restored in the mid-nineteenth century

62 Sir George Gilbert Scott was one of the most famous architects of the Gothic Revival. His design for the church of St Thomas of Canterbury in Parkgate Street, begun in 1869, was to have been topped by a tower and spire. The tower was never finished, leaving only a rather undignified stump instead

at Hastings, and retired to Chester to live in this cell as a hermit – though the evidence is somewhat flimsy.

There were once nine parish churches in the city, and while all of these churches have had interesting histories, this is seldom reflected in their architecture. All were either radically restored or totally rebuilt in the nineteenth century. Only St Mary's-on-the-Hill contains a substantial amount of medieval work, mainly of late fifteenth-century date and in the last true development of English Gothic – the Perpendicular. Some work of similar date survives in St Peter's, rebuilt, many times over the years. Its medieval spire was destroyed by lightning in 1782. St Michael's, virtually rebuilt around 1850 by James Harrison, retains a chancel roof of 1496. It now serves as the Heritage Centre, and its tower is unusual in having the end of the Row passing through it.

The insignificant-looking St Olave's in Lower Bridge Street

was one of a few English churches to be dedicated to a Norwegian king. Olave was killed in 1030 following his return home after fighting for the English. The church may have been founded to serve a small community of traders from the Norse settlement of Dublin, and had the smallest parish in the city. Described as unfit for worship at the start of the eighteenth century and as 'a low miserable building' in 1831, it was restored as a school in about 1860. Another chapel with a more eventful career is St Nicholas's, near the cathedral in St Werburgh's Street. Rebuilt at the end of the fifteenth century, it has since been adapted as a Commonhall, wool warehouse, theatre, music hall, cinema, supermarket and gents' outfitters.

Not surprisingly, most of the Victorian churches are Gothic Revival at its most impressive. The steepled piles of Holy Trinity, Watergate Street (by James Harrison, 1865–9, and now

64 Wales is only a stone's-throw from Chester, and the Welsh have always made up a large part of its population. One of several chapels catering for Welsh nonconformists is this Welsh Presbyterian church in St John's Street. Built to the designs of W. & G. Audsley of Liverpool in 1866, its most obvious feature is the huge rose window

the Guild Hall) and St Mary's-without-the-Walls, Handbridge (by F.B. Wade, 1885–7) are obvious landmarks in the townscape. Holy Trinity finishes off the view up from the Watergate, while St Mary's looks striking when viewed from the city side of the river. These would have been rivalled by John Douglas's Christ Church, Gloucester Street (1876 onwards) and Sir George Gilbert Scott's slightly earlier St Thomas of Canterbury in Parkgate Street – but in both cases the intended steeples were never built.

The wide variety of nonconformist religions were more varied in their architecture, using neo-classical as well as Gothic motifs. Among the better examples are the former Congregational church in Queen Street, rebuilt in 1838 and now part of a new supermarket development, and the Welsh Presbyterian church of 1866 in St John Street, designed by W. & G. Audsley with a

65 Not all churches aspired to architectural greatness to get their message across. Prefabricated buildings of corrugated iron sheeting were quite common at the end of the nineteenth, and early in the twentieth, centuries. A typical 'tin tabernacle' survives in Chester, and is now the Sealand Road United Reformed church

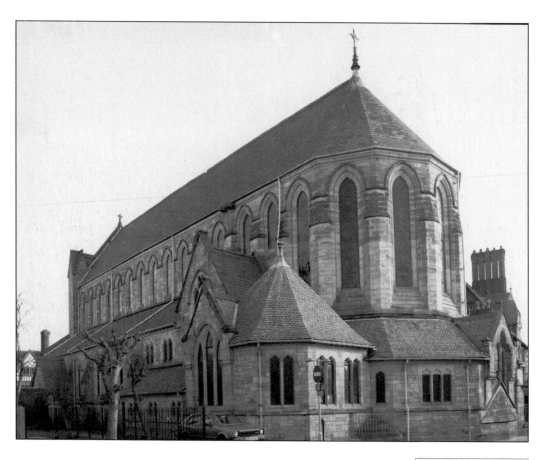

huge rose window. In many ways the most aesthetically pleasing of all the Victorian churches, not least because of its crisp, light-grey stonework and its simplicity of design, is the Roman Catholic church of St Werburgh's in Grosvenor Park Road. Designed by Edmund Kirby it was begun in 1873 but not completed until the west end was finally built in 1914; it too was originally meant to have a steeple.

66 The other St Werburgh's church in Chester is the third Roman Catholic church of that name – the first, of course, being the present cathedral. This fine church replaced a 1799 chapel, in Queen Street, and was designed by Edmund Kirby. Begun in 1873 it was finished just before the First World War

Public Buildings

As a key Roman stronghold, *Deva* would have had many important public buildings, but only the landscaped ruins of half the huge amphitheatre are visible. It was discovered purely by accident, when a workman was digging foundations for a new wing for the Ursuline Convent School in June 1929. Thirty years passed before any excavation could take place on the site. The amphitheatre is the largest to be found in Britain so far. It measured 314 ft by 286 ft overall, and the elliptical sanded arena was 190 ft long and 162 ft wide at its broadest.

Parts of the main headquarters building, the *principia*, have been found from time to time to the west of Northgate Street, and it had a colonnaded front some 244 ft long. Some columns of its north wing survive under No. 23 Northgate Street. To the north was the commander's house, under the forum complex and Town Hall, and a rock-cut *aerarium*, or strongroom, has been found in this area. Remains of the very extensive bath-house complex have also been found and a well-preserved *hypocaust* – an under-floor heating arrangement – lies beneath No. 39 Bridge Street. A good reconstruction of a hypocaust has been built in the Roman Gardens just outside the Newgate.

As an important regional centre since late Saxon times, Chester has always had administrative buildings. The early ones seem to have been rather ramshackle. In 1499 the Pentice was built alongside St Peter's church, governing the affairs of the street markets and housing the mayor and his officials among others. It was gradually superseded and the last vestiges of the building were pulled down in 1806. The disused St Nicholas's

67 The oldest public building in Chester is the ruined Roman amphitheatre just outside the Newgate. It was originally built in timber towards the end of the first century AD and rebuilt in stone shortly afterwards. Only half of the remains are visible. It could have held over 6,000 people and is the largest ever found in Britain

chapel was adapted in 1545 as a Common Hall, to hear local court cases, until 1698 when a new Exchange was built to cater for most of the city's administrators. That burnt down in 1862.

A competition for a new town hall was won by William H. Lynn of Belfast, and the foundation stone was laid in 1865. The huge neo-Gothic affair, of grey ashlared sandstone, was extravagantly decorated inside and out and cost the then massive sum of £40,000. It was officially opened by the future Edward VII, then Prince of Wales and Duke of Chester, on 14th October 1869. Next to the new Town Hall was the Market Hall, built in 1863 in a Baroque Revival style. This was knocked down in the late 1960s to make way for the hideous Forum complex and, to add insult to injury, a thin sliver of the old building has been allowed to remain for no obvious practical or aesthetic reason. The Shire Hall built by Harrison in the castle has been superseded by the

68 After the old Exchange was gutted in 1862 a competition to design a new town hall was started. The winner was the little-known William Henry Lynn of Belfast. The foundations were laid in 1865 and it opened in 1869. This huge grey sandstone Gothic pile, built in the mid-thirteenth-century style, has a certain Continental flavour but is effective mainly because of its sheer size. The tower is 160 ft high

County Hall, on the site of his gaol. Designed by E. Mainwairing Parkes, it was started in 1938 but the war delayed completion; it was opened by the Queen in 1957. This over-large, plain and rather tired-looking neo-Georgian affair was politely described by the inimitable Nikolaus Pevsner as 'not an ornament to the riverside view'. The county police headquarters, close to the entrance to the castle and opened ten years later, is arguably even less so.

As an important port Chester also needed a Customs House, and the present one, though no longer used for its original purpose, was built as late as 1868. In 1862 nearly £60,000 had been collected as revenue and 110 ships were registered as belonging to the city, although that usually meant that they were working from ports in the estuary – particularly Mostyn, on the Welsh bank. The mayor of Chester has, since the mid-fourteenth century, held the honorary title 'Admiral of the Dee'.

69 There was probably already a bridge over the Dee at the end of the Saxon era. Built of timber, it and the bridges that replaced it were swept away by floodwaters. The present masonry bridge was built between 1346 and 1358 by the royal mason, Master Henry of Snelsdon, but has been repaired many times since. It was widened on the east side in 1825-6 by Thomas Harrison, and tolls were still paid to cross it until 1884

70 The controversial county police headquarters, just outside the entrance to the castle, won a Civic Trust award. Designed by Edgar Taberner and built between 1964 and 1967, it cost over half a million pounds. The sculpted ends on the otherwise uninteresting block were designed by W. G. Mitchell, who poured liquid concrete on to polystyrene moulds to create this unusual effect

71 In the early nineteenth century the medieval bridge had become a bottleneck, and a new one designed by Thomas Harrison was built downstream. Built mainly of grey Peckforton stone, it cost £36,000, was opened by Princess Victoria in 1832, and its 200 ft long arch was claimed to be the longest single span of masonry in the world. Harrison died during its construction and it was finished by his pupil, William Cole

72 The first Queen's Park Bridge was opened in 1852 to link the new middle-class suburban development of Queen's Park, south of the river, with the city. It was designed by James Dredge of Bath. In 1923 a new bridge was built by David Rowell & Co. Ltd, in a style more typical of half a century before. It has a span of 277 ft

73 In 1717 the simple but elegant brick buildings of the Bluecoat School were built just outside the Northgate. The statue of the Bluecoat Boy over the entrance was put up as late as 1854. In the left-hand wing was the chapel of St John the Baptist, replacing an ancient one pulled down by the defenders during the Civil War

74 The Grosvenor Museum and School of Art, funded by the Duke of Westminster, was designed by Thomas Lockwood and opened in 1886. Grandiose and Gothic, it contains splendid Roman finds and excellent interpretative displays

Most large medieval religious foundations had schools attached to them, so Chester's educational history is a long one. Three school buildings of note survive, none of them particularly old and only one still in educational use. After the Dissolution, Henry VIII ordered the founding of new secular schools to make up for the loss of the monks. In 1541 this led to the creation of King's School, Chester for the teaching of '24 poor and friendless boys'. From the early seventeenth century they were taught in the former abbey's refectory. The numbers expanded and in 1876 a new school opened by the Abbey Gate, designed by one of the most respected architects of the time, Sir Arthur Blomfield. The school moved to just outside the city in 1960 and most of the old buildings are now used as a bank. A later bishop of Chester, John Bridgeman, founded the Blue Coat School in 1700, but it was not until 1717 that the buildings outside the

75 The Queen's School was founded in 1878 and in 1883 moved to these new premises on City Walls Road, designed by E.A. Ould. The brick decoration is carried out with skill and gusto, but it has to be said that the massing of the various components is somewhat uninspired

76 The Royal Infirmary on City Walls Road was opened to patients in 1759, thanks to a bequest from a Dr Stratford. In 1830 the exterior was remodelled by William Cole, and it has been extended several times since, notably in the early 1960s

77 The public library boasts a fine Edwardian Baroque façade on Northgate Street – all that is left of the former Westminster Coach and Motor Car Company works. Still in use as a car showroom at the start of the 1970s, the building was bought by a local arts group, but at the end of the 1970s work began on building the brand new library behind the restored façade

78 The swimming baths in Grosvenor Park Road bear the date 1900, and the typical mock-timber framing of Chester. They were designed by the firm of Douglas & Minshull

79 The former fire station in Northgate Street was opened in 1911 and was capable of taking three horse-drawn appliances. It was replaced by a new fire station in 1970. The building has rather pleasant rounded 'timber-framed' oriel windows – totally unhistorical but fun

80 Under the onslaught of television the cinema has taken something of a beating since the 1960s, and many have been pulled down or converted into bingo halls. Chester's Odeon has, happily, survived. Opened in 1936, its bold use of fluted brickwork is typical of the house style evolved by the firm's architect, Harry Weedon

81 Built on the site of the former Northgate railway station and opened in April 1977, the Northgate Arena is a multi-purpose sports arena with two swimming pools and plenty of other facilities. It is unashamedly modern and necessarily very large, but manages to be positive and progressive without being aggressive. Materials and scale are just right

Northgate were ready. They were built on part of the site of the medieval almshouses known as the Hospital of St John the Baptist. When the school was built, a new chapel of St John was incorporated into one of the projecting wings. The school closed in 1949. Unlike the King's School, the Queen's School has a much shorter pedigree. Founded in 1878 as the Chester School for Girls, it was allowed by Queen Victoria to call itself Queen's School and in 1883 moved to new premises on City Walls Road. These were designed by E.A. Ould, a pupil of John Douglas, and show obvious traces of the master's style in the ornately decorated brickwork.

Chester has one of the earliest public infirmaries still in use in the country. Founded in 1755 thanks to a bequest from a Dr Stratford, the brick-built complex on City Walls Road was opened for business in 1759, although only officially opened two years later. In 1783 it became the first hospital to build separate isolation wards for fever sufferers, and has been extended and added to ever since. In Chester it was perhaps inevitable that most public buildings at the turn of the century would be designed with mock-timber framing – and that even included the swimming baths of 1900 and the former fire station of 1911, both of which survive.

Houses

Up until the start of this century most people lived in the centre of towns. Many literally lived over the shop; others lived within walking distance of work or civic amenities; and the poor generally had no choice but to live in often squalid tenements and back alleys. All classes of society lived cheek by jowl and it was only in the eighteenth century that the gradual development of middle-and upper-class housing had begun. By the end of the nineteenth century the crowded and often unhygienic town centres were gradually abandoned by those who could afford to live in the new leafy suburbs, a process that has continued ever since. This has meant that the historic cores of places like Chester have lost some of their real character – and the amount of empty upper floors above otherwise busy shops is now causing concern.

Only tantalizing fragments of the domestic life of Roman Chester have come to light over the years. Very few of its inhabitants would have lived in houses, most being crowded into the barrack blocks occupying most of the town. Medieval remains are more numerous. Despite the Rows, the development of houses in Chester has, generally, been in line with that of similar historic towns. The Rows only really affected the front portion of the first floors of the houses and were accommodated into the designs. The first floors were simply the ground floors of any other town, the rest of the layouts being set out accordingly.

There appear to be no traces of any houses older than the late thirteenth century, which is hardly surprising given the amount of catastrophic fires the city experienced in the twelfth century. The earliest features that remain are the crypts (or undercrofts) under the Rows, and about two dozen of these date to the period between about 1280 and 1340. All are stone-lined, some had timber ceilings, but the better ones had, and some still have,

82 Although many medieval undercrofts survive in Chester and in many other historic towns, few of the medieval buildings that once stood above them do. If the Three Old Arches in Bridge Street are really late thirteenth-century in date, then this is one of the very few stone medieval house fronts left in any English town; most of the others are timber-framed

stone vaulting. The best examples are those under Nos 11 and 23 Watergate Street, No. 12 Bridge Street, and the aptly named Crypt Chambers in Eastgate Street. They were probably built by merchants as secure storage areas, and the grander ones may even have been used as a type of early showroom in which to display goods.

None of the medieval superstructures of these or any other of the crypts survive – apart from the stone arcade at No. 48 Bridge Street at the end of Scotch Row, well known as the Three Old Arches. They are dated to 1274, and if that date is correct these arches are an extremely rare survival of the front of a stone medieval town house. Life in medieval houses revolved around the hall, the largest apartment and the one used for living, eating and, originally, sleeping. Later, privacy became more important and separate sleeping accommodation became the rule. Only one

83 The medieval crypt under the mid-seventeenth-century timber-framed building at No. 12 Bridge Street was rediscovered in the mid-nineteenth century and cleared out. It is almost complete, with six bays of quadripartite vaulting – a type in which four vault ribs meet in the centre of each bay. Even its original late thirteenth-century windows and door survive. What better use for it today than a bookshop?

84 The oldest surviving intact medieval house in the city is the timber-framed Old Blue Bell, Northgate Street. It dates to the end of the fifteenth century. One unusual feature is the way in which the pavement runs right through the middle of the building. The 'cabin' at ground level between pavement and road was once a stage-coach office

85 The relatively unaltered framing of No. 77 Foregate Street is something of a relief after all the over-enthusiastic timber-framed revivalism of the city centre. Built shortly after 1600 this type of pattern is called herring-bone – for obvious reasons. The building once continued further to the right

86 Alderman John Leche was responsible for the modest seventeenth-century front of the Leche House, Watergate Street. It has been restored but has surprisingly kept the inserted eighteenth-century Georgian sashes. Behind the front range is a late fifteenth-century open hall, built over an earlier undercroft

87 Gamul House in Lower Bridge Street was derelict by the end of the 1960s and in danger of collapse. It was rescued by the city. Behind the rather unusual late seventeenth-century brick façade, with its oval upper windows, is a fine Jacobean timber-framed house. It was the home of Sir Francis Gamul, a Royalist, and Charles I is said to have stayed here in 1645

89 Bridge House was built or rebuilt for the attorney general of Cheshire, John Williams, in the early eighteenth century. It was then a symmetrical three-storey house of five bays, divided by pilasters. The slightly wider northern bay and the shops projecting in front of it are later additions

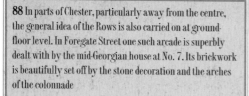

88 In parts of Chester, particularly away from the centre, the general idea of the Rows is also carried on at ground-floor level. In Foregate Street one such arcade is superbly dealt with by the mid-Georgian house at No. 7. Its brickwork is beautifully set off by the stone decoration and the arches of the colonnade

medieval hall survives to any great extent in Chester – a two bay, stone-built, early fourteenth-century example behind the front of Nos 40–2 Watergate Street. This hall runs parallel to the street and the owners clearly owned more than one of the narrow burgage plots so typical of medieval towns. A later hall nearby, still standing to its original height, is one of a series of rooms aligned at right angles to the street. The seventeenth-century front of the Leche House has a chamber on the second floor above the Row, but the undercroft probably dates to the fourteenth century and the hall to the late fifteenth. Gradually the hall became smaller and smaller as more and more functions within the house were given their own separate rooms. Eventually, in most houses, it was reduced to little more than a small access area or lobby.

Apart from these two houses in Watergate Street, and the late fifteenth-century Old Blue Bell in Northgate Street, most of the

(text continues on p. 101)

90 The remarkable Dutch House at the top end of Bridge Street, with its dramatically jettied bay windows and barley-sugar spirals, is unlike any other in Chester. This large three-gabled front dates to the mid-seventeenth century, but was radically restored in the early 1970s

91 Only six of the mid-seventeenth century 'Nine Houses' in Park Street survive. Built as almshouses, they have a masonry ground floor with a jettied timber-framed upper storey and were last restored in 1969

92 Booth Mansion, with its eight bays facing Watergate Street, is one of the largest Georgian houses in the city. Built in 1700 by Alderman George Booth it seems to incorporate much older work, and the arches over the Row could be medieval. It was once used as assembly rooms

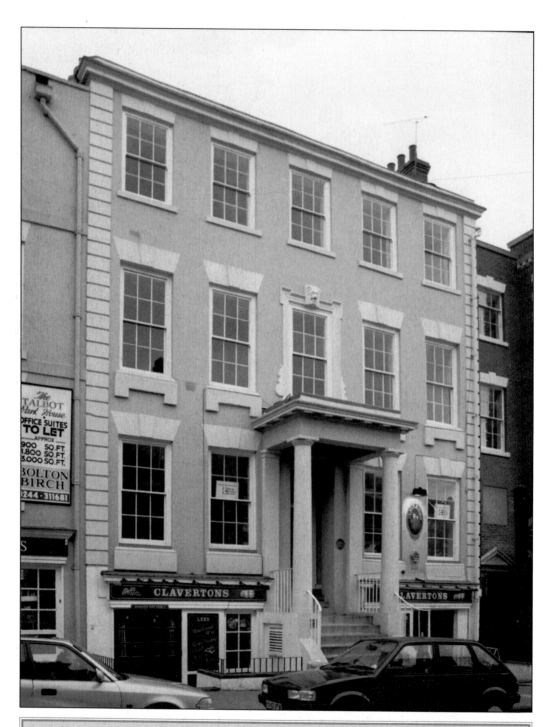

93 Park House, or the Talbot, was built in 1715, and by the early nineteenth century was known as the Albion Hotel. At that time it was an extremely popular venue and even had its own popular pleasure grounds to the rear, but these closed in 1865

94 Shipgate House is a fine late seventeenth-century brick town house on the corner of Lower Bridge Street and Shipgate Street. The overhanging eaves of the hipped roof are typical of the period, but it is likely that the sash windows were added later to replace casements. The house has recently been restored with considerable care

95 A typical early Georgian house, at No. 11 Whitefriars Street – simple but effective in design. The segmental arched-headed sash windows, the projecting brick string courses at first- and second-floor level, and the plain parapet hiding the roof are all typical of a style of architecture that has never really died out. Its proportions are pleasing and its detailing is good

96 Nos 4–28 Nicholas Street were built in 1781 by Joseph Turner, one time sheriff. This typical late Georgian brick terrace of identical three-storey houses with basements was nicknamed 'Pill-Box Promenade', because of all the doctors that once lived there. It has been rather cruelly cut off from the city centre by the inner ring road

10 Chester is a city that has thought about its road surfaces as well as its buildings. Soulless tarmac is held at bay. Abbey Square is a splendid example of how things should be done. The cobbles are well-preserved, and it has the added advantage of still having the flat stones, or 'wheelers', laid almost like the later railways, that prevented too much discomfort to the occupants of the rather basically sprung carriages of the eighteenth century

97 The owner of the end house of Stanley Place's south terrace certainly did not like getting wet. He built this charming sedan chair porch by his front door. With a door in each side wall, the sedan chair could be taken in from the street and the owner could dismount without being subjected to the vagaries of the weather. The chairmen, of course, were not so lucky

other houses in the city date from the late sixteenth century or after. By this time the standard domestic layout had virtually been set – with individual rooms for eating, 'withdrawing' and sleeping, as well as the usual service rooms such as the kitchens, larder, pantry and so forth. This has hardly changed since, except for the addition of bathrooms. Most of the changes in houses since the seventeenth century have been architectural, rather than functional.

One major change that did occur was the wide acceptance of the terraced house in the eighteenth century. Most houses before this had been built separately, even if they were packed tight in the same streetscape with other buildings. The building of long terraces started mainly in fashionable areas of London and Bath in the early eighteenth century and were copied in the rest of the country. Joseph Turner's 'Pill-Box' terrace in Nicholas Street is

(text continues on p. 107)

98 Tucked away off Love Street is one of the saddest Georgian houses in Chester. Forest House, probably built in the 1780s, must have been one of the grandest and had gardens to front and rear. These went in the early twentieth century, another building was built against it on the Love Street side, and the rest of the house was converted to a warehouse. It needs help – fast

99 Very few of the houses in the city centre have been left with large gardens. The Friars, off Whitefriars Street, is one of the lucky exceptions. The grounds were once occupied by a Carmelite priory. The house itself was built in two different stages during the eighteenth century

100 (top left) A splendid early eighteenth-century Palladian doorcase in Shipgate Street. **101** (top right) This remarkably plain door surround leads to No. 20 Castle Street, a late seventeenth-century house refaced in the early eighteenth. **102** (bottom left) The deanery in Abbey Street was built in 1764, and the neo-classical doorway is typical of its time. **103** (bottom right) The doorways to the houses of Joseph Turner's 1781 terrace in Nicholas Street are topped by fanlights and flanked by tall windows

104 In the early years of the nineteenth century brick went out of fashion, and many brick buildings were covered with stucco – a render lined to imitate stone. One of the few Chester examples, in Lower Bridge Street, and dating from the end of the Regency, also has rather delicate Gothick window tracery

105 The timber-framed revival began in Chester as early as the 1850s, and these two shops in Eastgate Street are the oldest examples left. Built in 1856 to the designs of Thomas Penson their detailing is fairly amateurish, but they are not as domineering as the buildings that were to come

16 Thomas Penson was far happier, and much more effective, when allowed to build in the Gothic Revival style, and it shows in his Crypt Chambers, Eastgate Street. This splendidly asymmetric stone pile was built in 1858 to a vaguely thirteenth-century Early English style to complement the fine medieval crypt below

106 Cleveland Place is a typical late nineteenth-century terrace, with houses for the better-off members of the artisan class but no unnecessary frills

the longest in Chester. Built in 1781 it was described as 'handsome modern brick buildings in the London style with sunken kitchens inclosed with a neat iron railing'.

Speculators quickly realized that terraces were cheaper to build than individual houses for the lesser classes too, and by the end of the century were building cheap terraces for working class families. This continued throughout the nineteenth century. Whole estates of terraced houses grew up outside the city walls, particularly in the Garden Lane, Newtown and Hoole areas to the north, served by their own schools and churches.

The cheapest form of housing was the tenement, common in most Scottish towns but a rarity in England. Chester has one of the few outside London. Parker's Building off Foregate Street was built for retired workers from the Eaton Estate, on the lines of some of the working-class flats being built by housing trusts

107 The terraced cottages of Lumley Place off Vicar's Lane were built in 1878. The simple but effective way in which the brick is used and the quality of design suggest the work of John Douglas

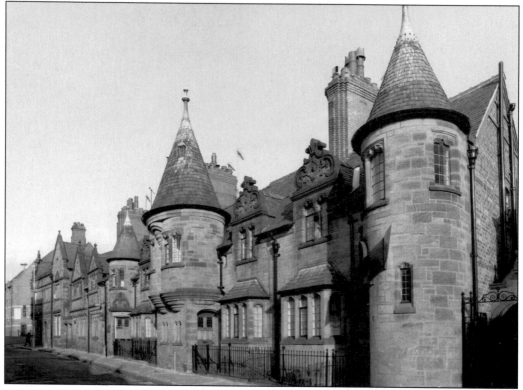

108 Eaton Hall, the home of the Grosvenors, is a good 3 miles from Chester but the family had their own tree-lined road between it and the outskirts of the city. This is Overleigh Lodge, in Handbridge, built in about 1893. The duke chose a London architect, R.W. Edis, and the design is neo-Jacobean

109 This delightfully eccentric stone-built row in Bath Street is by Douglas & Minshull and dates from 1902. It has everything – Scottish Baronial, Jacobean gables, a hint of French chateaux, and other bits simply dreamed up from nowhere. Architecture can be fun!

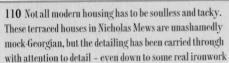

111 A new sheltered housing scheme by the Chester Canal, not far from the north-east corner of the city wall, has been thought out with some care. The buildings are modern, but on a human scale and built of traditional materials. The scheme deliberately faces away from the main road and towards the canal

110 Not all modern housing has to be soulless and tacky. These terraced houses in Nicholas Mews are unashamedly mock-Georgian, but the detailing has been carried through with attention to detail – even down to some real ironwork

in London. Built in 1888–9 to the designs of Douglas & Fordham (and clearly influenced by the brick style of John Douglas), the range provided very good quality housing for the time.

Chester even has its own garden suburb – albeit one that really failed to take off. Thomas Harrison laid out a new estate, patriotically called Queen's Park and designed for the wealthier middle classes, on the south side of the river in the 1850s. The sweeping roads were to be lined with large villas standing in their own spacious grounds, and the area was linked to the city by the new suspension bridge over the Dee. By the end of the century only a handful of houses had been built, but the streets have gradually filled up since.

In the early part of the twentieth century good quality council houses were built by the city. Later, in the 1960s, came the

112 Parker's Building, off Foregate Street, was put up to house retired workers from the Eaton Estate and was finished in 1889. Designed by Douglas & Fordham, the tenement form was copied from the work then being done by housing trusts in London to provide decent accommodation at affordable rents

dreaded high-rises – not many, but still too many. At least those in Chester have more breathing space than those in many an inner city. On the south bank of the river near the weir is a modern low-rise scheme, designed by Gilling, Dod and Partners – fairly unintrusive but, equally, fairly uninspiring. More recent developments in central Chester have, generally, shown a little more style. The redevelopment of St Mary's Hill by renovating the old and adding small-scale examples of the new has worked well. More ambitious schemes include Nicholas Mews, a row of obviously modern houses based on the well-considered pattern of a Georgian terrace.

Industrial Buildings

Chester's earliest industries were connected with servicing both the Roman and medieval garrisons, and with marketing the local agricultural produce. Roman *fabricae*, or workshops, have been located during excavations. In 1125 William of Malmesbury noticed that the locals enjoyed milk and butter, and that the rich ate meat – perhaps the first indications of the famous dairy and livestock industry of Cheshire. Fish from the river were also very important in the medieval economy, a fact that has continued to the twentieth century in the guise of Dee Salmon Fisheries on the Handbridge side of the river downstream of the weir.

The weir, or 'Causey', is usually attributed to Hugh Lupus. In the seventeenth century John Speed was not the only one to think that the reason for the silting of the Dee was 'the Sea being stopped to scour the River by a Causeway that thwarteth Dee at her bridge'. It channelled the river to power the waterwheels of the famous Dee Mills at the city end of the Dee bridge. These were in constant use, though rebuilt many times, until being burnt down for the last time in 1895. Such was the available water-power from the weir that at one stage there were six water-wheels in all used in grinding, two used to lift water to the city and three more for fulling. The water-power harnessed by the weir was still used afterwards to power the hydro-electricity plant built early in the twentieth century in their place.

One of the finest industrial buildings left in the city is also a flour mill – but a much later one that used steam power. Built in the late nineteenth century it also gave its name to Steam Mill Street, Boughton. This mill, and another further west along the

113 The Steam Mill, a large and elaborate exercise in ornate brickwork, ground flour, much of it brought in and taken away on the Chester Canal on whose banks it was built in the late nineteenth century. It has now been adapted to other purposes

114 The tall brick structure in the factory across the canal is not a chimney. It is one of the very few shot towers to survive in Europe and dates from the start of the nineteenth century. The firm of Walker Parker & Co. smelted lead and produced lead pipes

115 At the top of the short but steep Northgate flight of locks on the old Chester Canal is the lock-keeper's cottage. This may have been designed by Thomas Telford, engineer for the Ellesmere Canal Company, which amalgamated with the Chester Canal in 1813. Rather too close for comfort behind it is the inner ring road, opened in 1966

Chester Canal, have both found new uses – one a nightclub, the other an hotel.

Chester was once noted for making gloves and clay tobacco pipes, but few remains of the city's manufacturing past have survived. The most notable exception is on the opposite bank to the Steam Mill. The leadworks of Walker, Parker & Co. grew up at the start of the nineteenth century, and one of the surviving structures is the tall, circular shot tower. To produce lead shot, molten lead was taken up to the top of the tower and poured through a mesh. As they fell down to a tank of cold water at the bottom, the droplets of molten lead hardened into pellets. The Chester shot tower is one of only a handful left in Britain, and the best preserved of its date.

Chester's best industrial monuments are all connected with transport. The city has been an important transport centre since it

116 Tower Wharf was once a thriving inland port where boats from the Mersey and the Midlands met. Much quieter now, it still has some interesting canalside features, including a warehouse built partly over the water. This allowed barges to unload cargoes directly into it. To the left of the warehouses are the former Canal Company offices

117 The dry dock near Tower Wharf, where the summer-time river cruisers are repaired, is said to have been built as early as 1798, making it one of the oldest surviving examples on the canal system

was a Roman garrison at the end of the Watling Street – the Romans' main trunk route through England. Apart from a fragment of Roman quay wall in the Rodee, the Customs House in Watergate Street and the Water Tower in the defences, there are few reminders of how important a port Chester once was. It was also known for its shipbuilding. Celia Fiennes noted that 'they have a little dock and build shipps of 200 tunn I saw some on the stocks', and ships of this size were still being built until the 1920s in the western suburb of Saltney. Today only the name New Crane Street serves as a reminder of the eighteenth-century attempts to revive the port.

The remains of inland navigation are more substantial. The Chester Canal, which only went as far as Nantwich, was started in 1772 and the first section was open three years later. It was a commercial flop and was in danger of closing when it was effec-

119 Italianate architecture was all the rage, and popular with Prince Albert in particular, when Francis Thompson of Derby designed the magnificent façade of the General station. It opened in 1848 and was built by the four railway companies then serving Chester. Architecturally, it is one of the best on the whole system

118 The Chester Canal's dramatic cutting below the northern city wall was dug by pick and shovel in the 1770s and runs along the line of the original Roman fosse – the ditch outside the walls. In the background is the disused Bridge of Sighs, built by the canal company so that prisoners from Northgate gaol would not escape going to and from chapel in the Bluecoat School on the opposite side

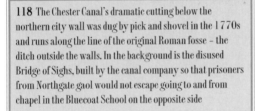

tively taken over by the Ellesmere Canal Company – an ambitious scheme attempting to unite the river Severn at Shrewsbury with the Dee and the Mersey. That larger company's line across the Wirral to the junction with the Chester Canal at Tower Wharf opened in 1796, but the junction was only completed a year later. This area now has some interesting relics. The Chester Canal drops down to the level of the Dee at the Northgate Locks, hewn out of the sandstone. At the top of the flight, originally of five but now of three locks, is a neat lock-keeper's cottage. This was probably added after the formation of the enlarged Ellesmere & Chester Company. At Tower Wharf itself is the Georgian headquarters of the canal company and, alongside, a warehouse built over the canal to allow boats to be loaded or unloaded directly beneath it – a typical Telford design. In the narrow piece of land between the canal and the short branch down to the Dee Basin is a dry dock, said to be an original structure of the 1790s. From Northgate Locks the old Chester Canal ran eastwards in a dramatic deep cutting right below the city wall. When the canal was being built the company had to guarantee that none of the prisoners in the gaol then in the old Northgate could escape in the confusion. Prisoners were later taken to St John the Baptist's chapel in the Bluecoat School over a private bridge that still survives, known as the 'Bridge of Sighs'.

The first railways to Chester were the lines to Crewe and to Birkenhead in 1840. The Chester & Holyhead opened its line along the north Wales coast in 1846. Both early stations were replaced in 1848 by a new joint station that also took Shrewsbury and Chester trains. This magnificent structure is one of the finest on the whole railway network, rivalling such masterpieces as York and King's Cross. Designed by Francis Thompson and built by Thomas Brassey, it has one of the longest façades in Europe. In 1874 a second station opened just outside the Northgate; this closed in 1969. Such was the complexity of amalgamations of lines in Chester that there were two different ways to get to London, with trains leaving the General station in completely opposite directions! After the 'groupings' of 1923 the city was served by trains of the London, Midland and Scottish, the Great Western, and the London and North Eastern companies, one of the few places outside London to have three of the four main line companies.

Further Reading

Local Books
Bethell, D., *Portrait of Chester* (1980)
Harris, B., *Chester* (1979)
Richards, R., *Old Cheshire Churches* (1974)
Seal, M., *Chester of Yester-Year* (1977)
Sylvester, D., *A History of Cheshire* (1971)

General Books
Brunskill, R.W., *Timber Building in Britain* (1985)
Brunskill, R.W., *Brick Building in Britain* (1990)
Clifton-Taylor, A., *The Pattern of English Building* (4th ed. 1987)
Cossons, N., *The BP Book of Industrial Archaeology* (1987)
Cruickshank, D.A., *A Guide to the Georgian Buildings of Britain & Ireland* (1985)
Harris, R., *Discovering Timber-Framed Buildings* (1978)
Pevsner, N., *The Buildings of England* series, in county volumes

Index

Page numbers in bold indicate illustrations.